West Chicago Public Library District
118 West Washington
West Chicago, IL 60185-2803
Phone # (630) 231-1552
Fax # (630) 231-1709

ROCKS: The Hard Facts

UNEARTHING SEDIMENTARY ROCKS

Willa Dee

PowerKiDS press

New York

For my friends at Herbertsville Elementary School

Published in 2014 by The Rosen Publishing Group, Inc.
29 East 21st Street, New York, NY 10010

First Edition

Editor: Jennifer Way
Book Design: Kate Vlachos
Photo Research: Katie Stryker

Photo Credits: Cover agap/Shutterstock.com; pp. 5, 7 by Greg Tucker; p. 6 iStockphoto/ Thinkstock; p. 8 (left) Mirenska Olga/Shutterstock.com; p. 8 (right) dexns/Shutterstock.com; p. 9 Dorling Kindersley RF/Thinkstock; p. 10 TTphoto/Shutterstock.com; p. 11 Neil A Rodrigues/ Shutterstock.com; p. 12 SeDmi/Shutterstock.com; p. 13 jacglad/Shutterstock.com; p. 14 Galyna Andrushko/Shutterstock.com; p. 15 (left) Adam Bies/Shutterstock.com; p. 15 (right) chomplearn/ Shutterstock.com; pp. 16, 17 salajean/Shutterstock.com; p. 18 cosma/Shutterstock.com; p. 21 Tomas1111/Shutterstock.com; p. 22 Leene/Shutterstock.com.

Publisher's Cataloging Data

Dee, Willa.
Unearthing sedimentary rocks / Willa Dee. — 1st ed. — New York : Power Kids Press, c2014
      p. cm. — (Rocks: the hard facts)
Includes an index.
ISBN: 978-1-4777-2900-7 (Library Binding) — ISBN: 978-1-4777-2989-2 (Paperback) — ISBN: 978-1-4777-3059-1 (6-pack)
1. Sedimentary rocks—Juvenile literature. 2. Rocks—Analysis—Juvenile literature. I. Title.
QE471.D44 2014
552.'5
Manufactured in the United States of America

CPSIA Compliance Information: Batch #W14PK4: For Further Information contact Rosen Publishing, New York, New York at 1-800-237-9932

CONTENTS

PRESSED DOWN

There are three kinds of rocks that make up our Earth. These are igneous rock, metamorphic rock, and sedimentary rock. Each of these rocks forms in a different way. However, all of Earth's rocks are made up of **minerals**.

Sedimentary rock forms when pieces of other rocks are pressed down and **cemented** together. It can also be formed from the **remains** of dead plants and animals.

Sedimentary rock is the most common rock found on Earth's surface. Layers of sedimentary rock make up the Grand Canyon. You can also find it in your classroom or on your kitchen table. Chalk is a kind of sedimentary rock. Table salt is as well!

You can see many layers of sedimentary rock in the Grand Canyon. There are almost 40 layers of sedimentary rock that built up on a base of metamorphic rock and that then eroded to form the canyon.

WHAT IS SEDIMENT?

Many rocks on Earth's surface seem very hard. However, wind and rain can slowly wear down rocks and break them into smaller pieces. Moving water or ice, such as rivers, floodwaters, ocean waves, or **glaciers**, can also wear away at rock. This process is called **erosion**.

The Narrows in the Zion National Park, in Utah, was created by erosion caused by the Virgin River. People who hike the Zion Narrows walk right through the river!

This picture shows sedimentary rock in Arizona. It has been eroded by water and wind.

As the wind or water moves, it carries away pieces of eroded rock. These pieces are called sediment.

Pieces of sediment can be large, like boulders, or small, like pebbles. Sediment can also be made up of tiny rock pieces that can only be seen through a **microscope**, such as grains of silt or clay!

FORMING LAYERS

Wind and water carry sediment with them as they move. When the wind or water slows down or stops moving, the sediment settles in a new place. The sediment forms into a layer where it settles.

Below: This picture shows sedimentary rock formations in Timna Valley, in Israel. When erosion breaks down this rock, it creates red, orange, and yellow sand. *Right*: You can see many strata in this rock face along the side of a cliff in Montenegro, in Europe.

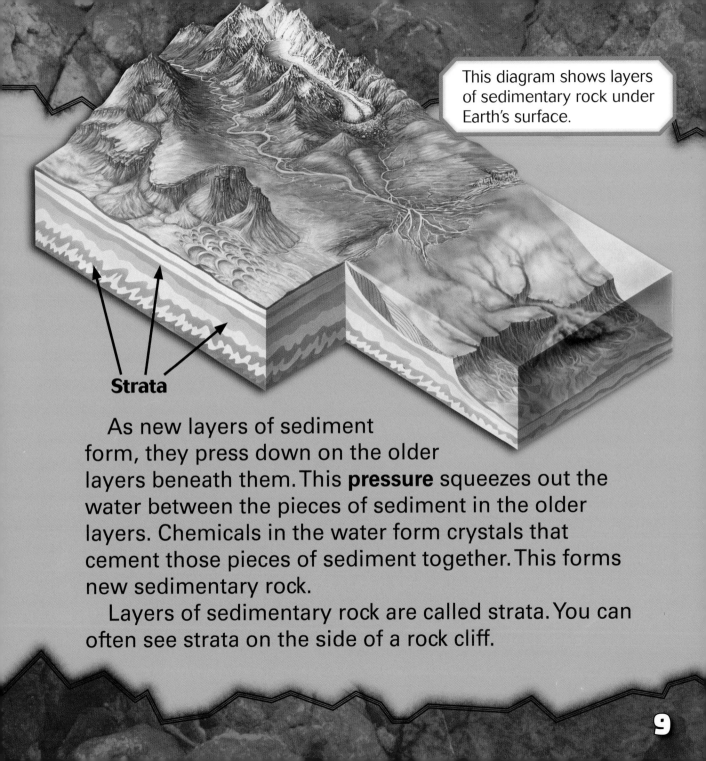

This diagram shows layers of sedimentary rock under Earth's surface.

Strata

As new layers of sediment form, they press down on the older layers beneath them. This **pressure** squeezes out the water between the pieces of sediment in the older layers. Chemicals in the water form crystals that cement those pieces of sediment together. This forms new sedimentary rock.

Layers of sedimentary rock are called strata. You can often see strata on the side of a rock cliff.

CLASTIC ROCK

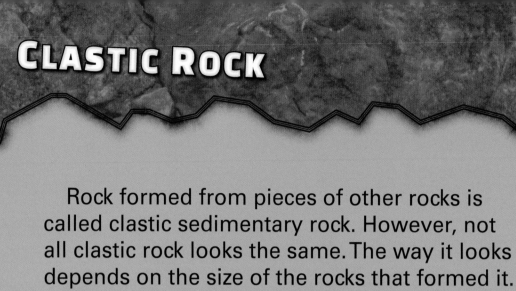

Rock formed from pieces of other rocks is called clastic sedimentary rock. However, not all clastic rock looks the same. The way it looks depends on the size of the rocks that formed it.

One common kind of clastic rock is sandstone. Sandstone is made from pieces of sand. Siltstone is another kind of rock, made from silt.

This picture shows shale, a clastic sedimentary rock. Shale is used to make paint, plastic, and bricks.

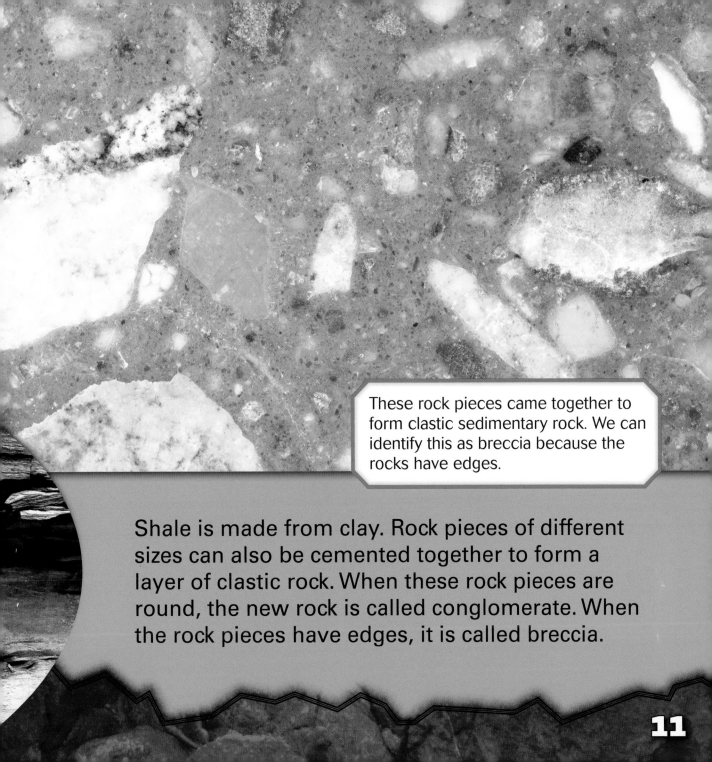

These rock pieces came together to form clastic sedimentary rock. We can identify this as breccia because the rocks have edges.

Shale is made from clay. Rock pieces of different sizes can also be cemented together to form a layer of clastic rock. When these rock pieces are round, the new rock is called conglomerate. When the rock pieces have edges, it is called breccia.

Another kind of rock is formed from the remains of dead animals or plants. This is called biological sedimentary rock.

When animals die, the soft parts of their bodies rot away. This leaves behind their bones and shells. Animal bones and shells contain minerals, as rocks do. The remains of dead plants are filled with carbon, another mineral.

Coal is a type of biological sedimentary rock. It is used for electricity and heat. China mines more coal than any other country in the world.

Chert is a kind of sedimentary rock. It can be used to start campfires.

Over time, bones, shells, or plant remains can pile up. These piles can be pressed into layers of biological rock. This can take millions of years!

Limestone is a common kind of biological rock. Limestone is formed from the shells of ocean animals.

CHEMICAL ROCK

Chemical rocks are another kind of sedimentary rock. When water moves through rock, it **dissolves** some of the minerals that make up the rock. Then, these minerals are carried away with the water.

When the water **evaporates** and **precipitates**, the minerals in the water can form into chemical sedimentary rocks.

You can see stalactites and stalagmites at the Carlsbad Cavern, in New Mexico. About half a million people visit the Carlsbad Caverns National Park every year.

Left: This picture shows stalactites and stalagmites in the Luray Caverns, in Virginia. The caverns were discovered in 1878. *Below*: This person is holding rock salt. Rock salt is made into smaller pieces before it is used as the kind of salt you put on your food.

Two common types of chemical rock are stalactites and stalagmites. These rocks form when water carrying **calcium** salts drips inside caves. Stalactites form at the top of the cave. Stalagmites form at the bottom. Rock salt is another kind of chemical rock. The table salt you sprinkle on your food comes from rock salt.

CLUES TO THE PAST

Earth is covered in oceans, rivers, lakes, deserts, mountains, and canyons. However, Earth's **landscape** has not always looked the way it looks today. Sedimentary rock helps scientists learn about what Earth may have looked like in the past.

These scientists are studying stalactites. Many stalactites are small, like these, but some people have seen stalactites that are more than 60 feet (18 m) long!

The scientists in this picture are studying a cave in Romania. They have found limestone, which means this cave might have been covered by an ocean years ago.

Sedimentary rock builds up in layers. The kind of sedimentary rock in a layer can tell us what Earth was like when the sediment settled there. For example, limestone found today may have been covered in ocean waters millions of years ago! When scientists find conglomerate rock, they know a river once flowed there. Sandstone shows where a beach or desert once was.

Scientists also can learn about past life on Earth from fossils. Fossils are the **preserved** remains of **prehistoric** plants and animals, such as dinosaurs. Fossils formed when layers of sediment covered plants and animals millions of years ago. Today, fossils are found inside sedimentary rock!

Scientists dig through layers of sedimentary rock looking for fossils.

This fossil of a lizard is a cast fossil. A mold fossil is formed when water breaks down an animal that is buried in rock. When a mold fossil fills with mud or sand, a cast fossil is formed.

This is a timeline of geologic time. As you can see, plants and other animals lived on Earth long before humans did!

The layer where a fossil is found can tell us how old the fossil is. Fossils show what the bones, teeth, and shells of prehistoric animals looked like. Scientists have also found fossils of leaf prints and footprints. Fossils help us study **extinct** life!

MILLIONS OF YEARS BEFORE PRESENT	PERIOD	REPRESENTATIVE LIFE
1½	Quaternary Period ↓	
	Tertiary Period	Primitive Horses
65		
	Cretaceous Period	Last Dinosaurs
140		
	Jurassic Period	Quarry Dinosaurs
210		
	Triassic Period	First Dinosaurs
245		
	Permian Period	Primitive Reptiles
290		
	Pennsylvanian Period	Giant Insects
320		
	Mississippian Period	Brachiopods
360		
	Devonian Period	Primitive Fish
410		
	Silurian Period	"Sea Scorpions"
440		
	Ordovician	Nautiloids
500		
	Cambrian Period	Trilobites
570		

Fossils older than Cambrian age are rare. This earlier span of time is usually called, simply, Precambrian.

FUELING OUR WORLD

Today, fossil fuels are used all over Earth to make energy. However, there are no dinosaur fossils in fossil fuels! In fact, the fossil fuel we use today was made long before dinosaurs walked the planet.

Fossil fuels come from the remains of plants and animals that lived hundreds of millions of years ago. After they died, layers of sedimentary rock covered their remains. Earth's heat and pressure helped change the remains into fossil fuels.

Oil and natural gas formed from the remains of plants and animals that lived in oceans and rivers. Coal formed from the remains of prehistoric forests and swamps.

This picture shows an oil refinery. At an oil refinery, fossil fuel oil is turned into gasoline, which is used to power cars.

PART OF THE CYCLE

Sedimentary rocks are all over Earth's surface. However, sedimentary rocks do not stay sedimentary rocks forever. Sedimentary rocks are part of Earth's rock cycle. Through this cycle, old rocks are broken down and new rocks form.

Over many years, sedimentary rocks can change into metamorphic rocks or igneous rocks. Metamorphic rocks and igneous rocks can also become sedimentary rocks. Erosion, heat, pressure, and melting are all things that change rocks from one kind into another. The rock cycle goes on forever!

You can see many layers of sedimentary rock in these cliffs in Arizona. Heat and pressure could turn this sedimentary rock into metamorphic rock. Weathering and erosion could turn it into sediment.

GLOSSARY

calcium (KAL-see-um) An element found in nature.

cemented (sih-MENT-ed) Brought together or made hard.

dissolves (dih-ZOLVZ) Breaks down.

erosion (ih-ROH-zhun) The wearing away of land over time.

evaporates (ih-VA-puh-rayts) Changes from a liquid to a gas.

extinct (ik-STINGKT) No longer existing.

glaciers (GLAY-shurz) Large masses of ice that move down mountains or along valleys.

landscape (LAND-skayp) The landforms, such as hills, mountains, and valleys, in an area.

microscope (MY-kruh-skohp) An instrument used to see very small things.

minerals (MIN-rulz) Natural matter that is not animals, plants, or other living things.

precipitates (prih-SIH-puh-tayts) Falls from the sky as moisture.

prehistoric (pree-his-TOR-ik) Having to do with the time before written history.

preserved (prih-ZURVD) Kept something from being lost or from going bad.

pressure (PREH-shur) A force that pushes on something.

remains (rih-MAYNZ) The parts left after a living thing has died.

INDEX

WEBSITES

Due to the changing nature of Internet links, PowerKids Press has developed an online list of websites related to the subject of this book. This site is updated regularly. Please use this link to access the list:
www.powerkidslinks.com/rthf/sedim/